High Jump as .　　　　.y

Gustav Parker Hibbett is a Black poet and essayist. They are originally from New Mexico and currently pursuing a PhD at Trinity College Dublin. They are a 2023 Obsidian Foundation Fellow and were selected as a runner-up for *The Missouri Review*'s 2022 Poem of the Year award. Their work appears in *Guernica, fourteen poems, The Stinging Fly, London Magazine, Adroit*, and elsewhere.

High Jump
as Icarus Story

Gustav Parker Hibbett

BANSHEE
PRESS

First published 2024 by Banshee Press
www.bansheepress.org

A CIP record for this title is available from the British Library.

Grateful acknowledgement is made to Seneca Review Books for permission to reproduce material from *Afterings* by Deborah Tall © 2016 Seneca
Review Books; and to Penguin Books Limited for permission to reproduce material from *American Sonnets for My Past and Future Assassin* by
Terrance Hayes © 2018 Penguin Books

Banshee Press gratefully acknowledges
the financial assistance of the Arts Council.

ISBN: 978-1-7393979-5-1

Set in Palatino by Eimear Ryan
Cover design by Anna Morrison
Printed in Ireland by Walsh Colour Print

For Abbie

Contents

High Jump as Icarus Story

I.

The curse of anyone nonwhite is that you are so busy arguing what you're not that you never arrive at what you are.

– Cathy Park Hong, *Minor Feelings*

Tortoise

Dream: you are a tortoise scaly-
limbed heavy-shelled tortoise
green clunky shell like old copper
a thing of tortoise beauty
toes like polished bits of plastic

you are however a jumper
among the tortoises it is you
who likes to push the vertical
legs stumpy as they are it's not
much but look it's something
to define yourself around isn't it

sometimes when you are alone you swear
you can get off-ground by inches
yes inches plural and maybe it's more
like centimetres at least that's what
the others say when they see you jumping
but you can swear you can really
swear that when you get going
you can see the ground like astronauts
see the lands and seas of Earth from space

you train with tortoise push-ups
and there isn't much room for arm
or leg muscles to bend but still
you bend them up and down and up
and down shell to the ground then back
as tall as you can stand shell up
against the blue lips of the sky

at night you fall asleep listening
to songs that are wet and slow
and smoky songs that move
like shifting sand in water songs
you dream yourself jumping out of
songs that look soft from above songs
you want to learn to read like tea leaves
like clouds or evening crow-flock shapes

Minotaur as Black Hole

You are something neither of your parents is,
though you look, in ways, like both of them,
like how adding red and yellow gives you
neither. Nuclear, how fusing elements creates
a different one, loses little subatomic pieces.
You are mass compacted after supernova,
self that cancels out itself. Light, your bedroom,
is where language goes to mutate. Auto-cannibal,
to see yourself reflected at close range.
To look for safety in your eyes just to find
that bleaching gaze, dissecting. In the constellated
darkness, slice yourself apart with hierarchies.
Black's what suns define themselves against,
so they hold their skin against your gravity,
comparing swatches. Everything you swallow
sets up shop inside you. Contradictory,
self-devouring, autoimmune, all you want is
legibility. Because *you're still*. But *you aren't like.*
They examine you with taxonomic telescopes.
Okay but like what are you? Everyone's genetics
project. Site of all their horrors, fantasies.
Even as you watch yourself you morph.

High Jump as Flow State

By some accounts, I was an artist
above the crossbar, pure potential.
Coaches from other places would
approach my dad at State, tell him

with that form they'd have me jumping
six, eight inches higher within months
if I went and trained with them,
though it was never possible

for me to quit my life and study
high jump as an altered state of being.
Still, all I cared about for years
was how my body moved over the bar,

my mind's eye annotating energy
with cartoon physics diagrams,
from run to planted foot to torso,
diverted up and back and over,

devotee to the feeling – diamond
needle in a record's groove – that
anything worth doing is worth doing
beautifully. Most nights before bed

I'd watch YouTube compilations
of the perfect form, slowed down
so I could see the moment when
the jumpers flipped their heads back:

oftentimes they'd close their eyes
until their legs cleared, the language
of this prayer a special privacy between
the jumper and their own ambitions.

Quickly and Quietly

We are late for Sunday school
when we pull up in our awkward
church clothes – khakis, button-
downs, and dresses; curls greased
and flattened or in tidy braids –
Bobby Caldwell's voice still playing
as we open doors, grab Bibles.
It's not a Black church, just
the best Albuquerque can do,
but Dad has never found a temple
he can't worship in. As he locks the car,
he reminds us to go *quickly and quietly.*
Repeats it like an incantation: *quickly and
quietly.* A prayer, maybe. He says this
all the time, so we've already learned
to wear it like an heirloom. *Quickly
and quietly.* We understand already
what it means to make our bodies
an apology: this is a way of living.
Silent, heads bent slightly, we go
into church. *Quickly and quietly,*
Dad says one last time as we move
to find our rooms, our seats,
this time like a champagne bottle
smashed against a brand-new ship:
a blessing. *May the water part
for you. May you survive it.*

Archaeopteryx

Often, you are your own coach.
You have a lot to learn about bodies
in motion. For example: arching
has to start at the neck; torso
follows like an arrow shaft.
Or: if you train your core,
you can make your energy change direction
mid-air, preserve it from your run,
or from the little one-leg crouch
before your jump. You watch videos
of others jumping, imprint their motions
on your mind so much that when you sleep,
you see their bodies on your retinas.

Diversity Statement (500 words)

In the years that formed me, I poured myself into classes, hobbies, extracurriculars I was told you'd like: Latin, Mandarin, Multivariable Calculus, Swimming, AP Physics. Until everything about me summarized to fit a single sheet of paper. I trimmed myself, and now you only want the trimmings. I could tell you about this, if you want. How much energy I spent on minimizing, how I dreamed that someday they'd only see me when I wanted them to. How I thought I had to empty myself in order to be refilled. How half-white meant the mask stayed mostly on at home. How one time my favourite teacher told me I looked angry just because she couldn't see my mouth. How it felt to have parents who compounded this, because they wanted so badly for me to make it more than they did. How they believed in this school so much they drove all the way across town twice a day so we could go there, and how they leveraged this against us any time we failed to redefine perfection. How for years, the only time I felt alive was in the air, when I was high jumping. So much so that when I saw that movie *Ice Princess*, all I wanted was to jump just like she ice-skated, how she taught herself to silence competitions with her grace, until the way her body moved turned into something clean, objective, definite that let her earn respect and keep on going, until her skate routines had whole rinks on their feet. Until her academic mother let her choose it over Harvard. In the four months of the year that the high jump mat was out, I would stay out at the track, long after practice ended, just jumping. I set up a bungee so it didn't fall, and ran and jumped and ran and jumped and ran and jumped, until I couldn't get up off the mat. I can tell you how I knew with every molecule that high jump was a sport that I could only access if I kept on winning, if I stayed good enough to stay on teams. How I'd never get that access otherwise. How I drove myself to injury after injury and still I kept on jumping injured. Won injured. How I made a name for myself in New Mexico, won meet after meet, and kept on pushing because I still wasn't good enough for Stanford. How I never made it high enough and chose to go there anyway, and how that broke my heart. How often I was asked, still, if I was admitted as an athlete, like I was a body that only happened to have a head attached to it. How I've never felt anything as good as flying feels, and how I know I never will again.

Other People's Fear Keeps Me Up at Night

after Morgan Parker

At the train station, there is a church bell
ringing in my chest, or trying to. Muffled

clapper reaching out for one lip then the other,
striking only leather. A man has stopped me

getting off the train to Kansas City,
and the river of the other passengers

is passing noiselessly around me,
the island of my suitcase open,

spilling clothes and books and sleeping
bag onto the platform. I am not allowed

to touch, like at the airport, so I watch
him root, untidy everything. *Just in case*

you're bringing drugs or something. He calls over
another man, a search dog, while every other

passenger flows past me. While we wait,
he asks me if I go to college at the institution

stamped across my sweatshirt, won't believe me
when I tell him *yes, I do*. Twinkles like he's caught me

in a lie. It's mid-August, so I should be there
already. Now he wants to take my sleeping bag

out of its stuff sack. I try to tell him that we start
in late September, but there's something in my chest

that keeps on stopping short of sound. Prayer
that goes to kneel and keeps on falling, keeps on

finding nothing solid. I could be lying,
could be anything he says I am.

It's two weeks since Michael Brown.
My hands are shaking, but he almost smiles

when he tells me he might need
to take me to his office, easy

as someone might tell me that it's raining,
that they might be having casserole for dinner.

up the staircase   there are   walls of touch

massive tables spread   with diagrams in black

stained   and decorated

the librarian curator   unfurls

walks us through   the cartographic whimsy

and its monsters   beasts

or just one giant foot

hunger   shadows

flickers

silhouettes   against the paper

how space is narrowed   into sense   or

how to   sketch something

and certain as the sun

to set the axis

how

map room

screens   glass   and wire-front bookshelves

and white   and faded colour   coffee

with the ink of empire

history

of medieval Britain

with faces   in their chests

or snouts for heads   or no mouths   no human

 in the flame's corona   when a candle

and goes   smoky

skin   of eyelids

journey into memory

and make it   stiff

how to nest   the universe

 on a nation's pen   ptolemaic

to script a globe's phrenology   and spin it

In Which I Dream That I Sing Like Lianne La Havas

In 'Ghost', there is a staircase Lianne climbs;
spiralled, gilded, effortless; royalty on their way

to bed; earthy marble steps in rabbit slippers.
A voice entitled to itself, to ease. I dream,

one night, that I am singing along to this,
my notes there next to hers. A palace guest,

I am timid but accurate, a shadow sidecar
on her sheet music while she walks the halls

with nowhere else to be. She stays, until
the crescendo, in my range – and I manage

mimicking everything except her ease,
the carefree way her timbre drapes a robe

across its shoulders. On the first chorus,
she takes the first few steps: up a few,

then back down. Poses sitting with a hand
across her forehead, head leaned backwards.

And I follow in these acrobatics, near the best
I've ever been when I'm awake. I almost believe

that I belong here, cloaked in opulence, pearled
with grace notes. But the next chorus comes

soon after the first one. At the stairs already,
she turns to climb. I have only ever stopped,

dropped an octave here and matched her motions
from the ground floor, shadow cast across a fall.

But this time, I begin with her, *always with the ghosts
of us in tow*, swooning at the base of the stairs,

and when she starts to climb my voice moves
with her, *is* her. Clad in femme divinity, I am

grand and satiated shameless, celebrated
without need to be; my triumph like the time

a ballet dancer takes to float before they land.
Until I wake, I've proven everything I ever

needed to. My performance here is not a ticket
into more rooms I will have to sing to stay in.

High Jump as Religious Calling

Prayer, like anything, takes practice.
To put your back to a bar and jump
without looking, bend your knees
and bend them again, feel without
touching, without turning back to look.

Trust, like anything, takes practice.
You're the kid who always sits where
they can see a room, and knows the exits.
Learn to move like a marionette
pulled up at the waist by a string,
up and slightly back, almost forgetting
what's behind you. Up, then back.
Practise holding this position: arms
and forehead up and backward,
pelvis lifted skyward. Eyes shut,
memorize the arc your body makes.

Back-overs, like anything, take practice.
Submit yourself to muscle memory,
until trust replaces knowing. Liquid,
head thrown backwards, floating:
you begin each practice like this.

grendel

i.
when   laura marling sings   that   there are

   lonely beast[s]   *[that need]*   *defend[ing]*   the first

         beast   i think about   is grendel

   armless   slinking back   across

the moors   to tell his mother   golden

   hero beowulf   came all this way   to send him

         to whatever heaven   monsters go to

   look: there's something   three-fifths

human   about a body   made to bear   the fears

   of other people   slipping   out of sight

         to die   at home   /   ending   his myth

   with what he is   to himself   his mother

i don't know   how   to say this

   in my early english lit class   so i wait

to boil over   in section   the day   after

my professor   teaches caliban   only

through the way   he hurts   miranda

so that he   remains   invisible   to us

before   and after   he gets   violent

as if it is   caliban's   desire   for a future

island   populated just by   beasts   who look like him

that is the   locus   of the tempest's   savagery

ii.
the moment   rittenhouse   unloads   his ar-15

i know   he will become   a folklore   hero

and i tell   the white man   at the   only

therapy   screening   i am able to afford

that these days   i can see   america

so clearly   it keeps me   from   sleeping

resists   every rest-inducing   drug

that i can't take   anything   in good faith

    anymore   because i've   stopped believing

the   people   of this country   don't

    understand   exactly   what it is

they're doing   /   that i'm   angriest

    about believing   them   making   excuses

for them   while all they really   wanted

    was to cleanse their   story   of the monster

of me   /   the man says   i have a problem

    with overthinking   there's been   unrest

before   he says   will be   again and   what

    we need   to do is think   about how   *lucky*

we are   to live   in this time   this moment

    with its sun   its bees   and flowers

After Practice, a Black Boy Goes Supernova

for Noah

Beauty is not a luxury; rather it is a way of creating possibility …
       – Saidiya Hartman, *Wayward Lives, Beautiful Experiments*

It's evening, and the grass is gathering
cold. We are the last two on the track,
silhouetted underneath the football field
uprights, not ready for the heat to leave us.

The high jump mat is webbed in shadows
growing deeper every moment – soon
the light will be too thin for trying; soon
we'll stow the bar and standards, replace

the cover on the mat, unlace our spikes,
and slip into our night-time trivialities,
disappear into the dulling of an institution
that will mistake us for each other,

but for now we set the bar above the heights
we understand, allow ourselves each one last
attempt. The germinating dark is silent
but for crickets; we are each other's only

witnesses. We understand like no one else does
how it feels to be a body hanging, burning
in the space between. Interchangeable,
disposable. We know that when they see us

they see both, or neither. At meets, they call us
the *high jump brothers,* ask us if we're maybe twins
or cousins. Tonight, I jump first. A few
false starts, and then I'm off, elastic-smooth,

determined, wondering what it'd be like
to clear this height with no one here to know
but us. To claim it: *yes, I've cleared six-eight.*
But I miss – unmoor it with my shoulder,

though as we set it up again Noah assures me
I was over it. Just a matter of alignment,
of fine-tuning. Now he takes his mark.
Pauses for a moment, then starts bounding,

slowly curving, making tighter, smaller steps,
keeping something headlong, something
starter pistol in his stride, then up.
A sail full with sudden wind. An exhale

of an upward motion. Turning as he rises,
blooms. His head clears, then his torso, then
his calves. He clips it with his heels, his kick
a millisecond slow, but it's clear this height belongs

to him. Given time, given another run, another
jump like that. His. His body and the bar start falling,
then they stop mid-air. Something in the fabric
of the evening splits open. Time implodes,

and at its centre, Noah, in the air above the mat,
going supernova; full of everything he ever wanted,
everything he didn't: protostars and space clouds,
black holes and pulsar winds. Laws of man

undone, rewritten around cotton candy swirls
of gravity and colour. Black boy as anything,
as the music of an inner world inside out.
I see galaxies erupting, life reforming.

Planets where the word for *dark* means *sacred*.
Worlds where we move like we move
in the air, unbound. Then he lands, and things
compose themselves again. Stars unborn.

Shockwaves in reverse, until the world
is how it was, though we felt it change.
We saw it rearrange itself.
We saw the world rearrange itself for us.

Othello as Singer-Songwriter

The real Othello is dark, long-eyelash pretty.
He dangles daily statements from both ears, manifests
his strength as tenderness. And he loves his Desdemona
passionate – no need for jealousy. He's complex,

contradicts himself, is human. If you catch him
when he thinks there's no one watching, you can see him
whimsical, between the Venice waterways at night,
crouched to watch the lamplight bleed like fire spilled

across a floor of oil. In his spare time, when he's not
our great commander, he writes lyrics, and believes
that if he'd had the choice he'd be a troubadour, a man
who turns the texture of his madness into music.

Fancies that his voice, someday, will hold a baritone
so velvet-rich, so soft, we'll know him just for that.

What I Would Have Wanted Fleabag to Say for Me, Had the Priest Not Brought It Back to Sex

… and there's a dread I feel I've held close
forever, and I want to be told how to lose it,
to let it fall like cliff faces ease themselves
into the ocean, but I think my morality
is tied in with internal anti-Blackness
in a knot I can't untangle. And Father,
sometimes I feel guilty just for breathing.

I'm Prometheus chained to the rock, by my own
hand this time, and guilt is the eagle ripping through
my abdomen. He is rooting in me for my liver,
but it's *shame* he finds, coiled biblical and,
hungry, he pulls. *The way my eyes look wild*
when I'm angry. Or how I am behind a phone,
obsequious and false and jiggy. Father, listen.

I'm a bad son, and I'm selfish, with attachments
formed for gain. There's something poisonous in me
that I've never opened up to show, and I want
for you to tell me how to fix this. How to tell
the people who see good in me there's nothing
underneath it. That there's this snake. And *maybe*
I shrank from masculinity because I was afraid

of being Black, or now I'm bad at being Black
because I let them tell me what Black is,
and part of me knew I'd always prove them right.
Father, I'm the kind of beast that eats itself; the snake
the eagle finds is always headless. I want someone to tell me

how to cleanse this, and Father, *when I have sex, I beg*
to be unravelled, because I know no one will ever really

absolve me how I need it. Something more than skin
is naked now in front of you, and I'm asking you
to shape it into order. Kill the snake or tame it,
or rewrite the snake as righteous. How is it okay
that I betrayed myself the way I did? What wants
am I allowed to have? Show me how to hold
the pleasure I am jealous of; show me peace.

II.

Inside me is a black-eyed animal
Bracing in a small stall. As if a bird
Could grow without breaking its shell.

– Terrance Hayes, *American Sonnets for My Past and*
Future Assassin

Joni Mitchell dresses up as me

Dark-felt fedora and sunglasses;
little black-haired moustache; afro
wig; skin the hue of walnut wood
painted over face, neck, hands;
gold chains; earrings; jewel-toned
blazer – I am the sort of man
an artist wears to sing in, dons
to shed herself: puffed-up,
pimpin', perfectly impermanent.
I am beautiful, she says: the wisp
of something Negro in the twilight
timbre of her mezzo, piano riff
of blackbird wings, noble sorrow
turned arpeggio. My brass
bravado grand enough
to make her troubles soulful
jewellery, leave her feeling
freer, deeper, natural. She loves
that I'm the friend she's never had
to worry for, the man who jives and jukes
so centrifugal that my noose is dewdrops
slipping from a crocus stem, who grooves
so fast the cops can't catch
my saxophone. Seductive, tragic,
lovely, Joni says she loves my self-
possession, how it feels
to possess me.

High Jump as Divination

The second-last step is the most
important. There are said to be
those who can tell if someone's
gonna clear their jump just by watching

the way their body dips, how much
upward force they generate,
the angle of their planted knee.
It's crucial, make or break:

how you get down governs
how you fly; you either leave
with wings or you stay human,
decided in the moment just before

the moment. You take videos
of yourself, cut them off before
the jump, then scramble them
so you can't remember which result

each run-up led to. Watch your yellow
jumping shoes hit the mark again
and again, until you blur into a queue
of selves in uniform. A tense flutter

of shoelaces. Halo of dust dislodged,
like a moonwalker. Learn to read
this language like a kind of augur.
You'll either make it or you won't.

Personal Mythology

In our rented Nissan Maxima, we are slowly headed east,
though I'm not sure yet if that means back or forwards.
I am showing you the soul of me, or we are searching
for it, in the storms and desert highways of New Mexico.

I can't remember a time I didn't want to leave, and yet
somehow I'm back. I knew the Pledge both in English
and in Spanish, used to recite it over the intercom
in elementary school, and yet neither *para todos* nor

for all seemed meant for me, so I dreamed one day
I'd slip beneath the water of another country's
population. Assimilation as surrender, as peace.
And yet somehow I'm back, unsatisfied. Born again

American, this time on my terms. As we drive through
wind, through dust storms, I point out my own holy places:
I used to bike alongside that arroyo, super-charged with speed
from the hill that fed into it, holding on for dear life,

though I never fell. Or: I practised soccer here, before
they paved it over, once jumped so high for a chest trap
that my feet cleared my teammate's head. Or the summer
my brother and I became explorers on our longboards,

coursed through westside neighbourhoods like lightning.
How my family moved here first on the fourth of July,
and how each year we'd pilgrim to our hilltop, watch
every fireworks show the city had to offer all at once,

call out the best explosions using places instead of clock
face numbers: Balloon Fiesta, Rio Rancho, Isotopes,
South Valley. Stayed until the sky fell quiet. All the things
I never thought I would remember, eager as I was

to flush out, rinse, refill my history. *Wise men still seek
Him*, a roadside church marquee tells us, and though *them*
feels much more accurate to me these days, I've learned lately
that if paradigms don't fit, it's okay to customize them.

Pink

In a story that my mother likes to tell, I am a toddler in a shoe store. Small in front of so much splendour, I'm a raven overwhelmed by shimmer. Shelves filled with possibility that has yet to actualize, potential energy that has not yet been directed. Wonder. Neither do I understand the limits of money. I haven't yet built up the caution I have now, where what I want is filtered first through what is feasible; and so I stand inside a store of what I only see as choices. Pleasures. Wealth is really most about its choices, the doors they haven't closed on you. As my mother tells it, I am drawn immediately to one pair: pink and shiny. In reconstructing memory, I picture them as velcro, made from that matte plastic fabric that holds shimmer like a prism or a puddle at the gas station. And I can see myself in them: flashy, unselfconscious, in a piece of art I like and therefore want to carry with me. A glass pebble taken from the beach for rolling in my palm, and then returning to my pocket. The private sort of smoothness, meant for no one else but me. But there is a context past the boundaries of my consciousness, and I am overruled. My mother understands, as I do not, what this choice will tell the world about me, and she herself is not prepared to claim it. That I am Other, even beyond my skin tone, in ways I will need years to understand, defend; longer still to own. In my innocence, the world is mine to summit. Any of these shoes are mine, or can be.

Tetris

i.

Our computer was upstairs
in that house. High-ceilinged
living room, kitchen off at one end;
upstairs, always bright and blue and open.

I couldn't read back then, and in the mornings
I would rise to find my mother at the keyboard
in the open air at the top of the stairs,
taking news from the black and white
on the glowing screen. Breakfast then,
and the computer still a mystery
I couldn't access. She called it
a gateway to the world, and to me
she was its keeper. Sometimes

she used this power to play Tetris,
and I'd come and watch the blocks
and how they fell. Colours and squares
folding together in some strategy
I couldn't fully comprehend.
She moved them like she kneaded
dough, with a sure, decisive hand.

ii.

Soon, my game felt fluent,
bonuses and exploding blocks
lighting up the screen like Christmas.
Here was a language we now shared,
a brand-new tongue I'd taught myself
to speak so quickly. I was proud,

but the face she made told me
she hadn't meant to share this.
I'd trespassed, hurt her by making it,
in part, my own. She played slower;
it was less about the scores
than it was about the quiet
that it brought her.

She made the same face
when the books I chose to read
were different than the ones
she would have, but still I kept on
choosing them, kept on driving my life
outside the scope of her intentions,
and I soon forgot how our computer's
glowing text appeared to me
those mornings, in the open
blue-strung light of childhood:
like the gateway to her world.

High Jump as the Kind of Painting It Burns to Stand in Front of

The art of flight is not so mundane
a thing as squats or the silly masculinity
of deadlifts, though you must go through the
motions in the weight room anyway. Otherwise,
you prefer to be a body unrestrained, so you focus
most on things like box jumps, jump rope; exercise
that stirs a little whimsy in with the hard work, shows
you're more than just a body. Math was where you used
to do this, where numbers and their rules were evidence
that you were just as smart as any other student, but now
your Calculus BC teacher calls you a 'slacker', sneers at you
when handing back a barely passing grade, needles cruelly
when you're brave enough to stop by office hours, even
though you've never worked as hard for any other class,
so now you've had to learn that math will not protect
you, that math isn't safe, isn't nearly as objective
as it seems. Now it's only in the air you feel
greater than the sum of all your efforts,
so you're careful not to kill this. Afraid
if you look too closely at your high
jumping, you'll make it vanish.
If you're good enough at this,
you won't lose it. If you're
good enough, you'll get
to keep on jumping
till your back
gives out.

High Jump as Life Lessons

i.

you insist on starting every practice   with your back

        against the bar   to see   what you can do   without

the things you take   for granted:

                                your run-up   speed

                                your patterns

                                or your sight

            in fact   for back-overs   it's best to close your eyes

                before you jump   embrace praying

            with your head bent   backwards

train yourself   not to turn around   and peek

your form   is at its purest   here   it's just the jump

    the bend   the timing   then   the cloud of   dust

your body dandelions   when you hit   the mat   this should

feel like   submission   should feel like a body   ruled by breath   by sublime   quiet

you are building something   that will take you   stratospheric

so it's best   to make the fundamentals   a religion

ii.

you have another game   that's called   endurance
where you hang   a bungee   need three perfect
clears   before you move it   up   two inches
then assign   yourself   three clears   again
  again   each time   you hit the bungee   add
  another   necessary   perfect clear   before
    advancing   soon   you need   five
     or six   before you can move on   the only
      breaks you get   are in the time   it takes
       to raise   the bungee   you'll   grow
        to love the   obdurate   the sickness
         of atoning   for your body's anaerobic
         shortcomings   crave   the simple
          cruelty of   becoming   your own
           punisher   the master   of your own
           exhaustion   knowing just   how far
            to push   before you're   spent
             before   you get to be   the
              one   to show   yourself
                some   mercy

Rococo

for Abbie

ornamented into motion, like a dancer paintbrush-cast in costume
in the background of a *fête galante*, like the way you wake up
    into dreams,
i'm *somewhere* without knowing how i got here. clouds fluffed
    pink,
skies as sinuous and rolling as they are in fresco. taken by surprise
and i'm still finding bearing; from here, the pastel fields of
    lavender
seem to stretch forever, all directions. *trompe l'œil* breeze – real,
    now,
as brush on gessoed canvas – warm against my cheek.

and what i mean by this, all this, is that i'm lucky – these days,
when i find my world falling, this is always where it lands.
some nights in dreams, i see your lilied figure spread above me
on the ceiling, a better place's favourite goddess. a deity who
    always answers
prayers, with ears for only mine. in the holied sea foam of your
    eyes,
in the early morning trumpets of your voice, i find my
    absolution. just,
i need for you to understand the way it felt for me to be nowhere,
and then – with you – such a rosy, stunning *somewhere*, suddenly.

On Beauty

With beauty, something is always at stake.
— Christina Sharpe, *Ordinary Notes*

There are times I want to take adult ballet classes
simply because I'm caught up in how good
I'd look in *grand jeté,* how beautiful it'd be to land
and step immediately into the kind of turn
dancers make with hands above their heads,
night-bloom flowers with their moonlit petals
spilling open. I've always had a thing for spinning
when I dance, for acting as though this and this
alone will make me happy. To stop the world static
like a VHS on pause, a grey-black space station
in zero gravity, an exoplanet twirling on a tidy axis.
Delicate, invincible. Fingertips up straight, palms
flat together, wrists wound once around each other,
arms falling as I spin, grand unfolding
lotus, clarity exonerated of a self.

Lunar Cycle

My father texts me every full moon, and it almost always goes unanswered, because I don't know what to say. It was him who showed me how to excise sentiment, not by teaching but by example, lest it interrupt the work I had to do – the math test *As* he wanted turned into *A+es*, the dismissive threat to send me to what he called *Problem-Solving Camp* every time I couldn't figure something out myself – and perhaps I'm bitter that he's the one sending sentiments I don't know how to reply to. Such that I am the cold one: too practical, too stressed. Inaccessible. They who have no need for feeling unless it comes convenient. Who taught themself to jar it, to open only when it serves a purpose. Who leaves these texts unanswered, month after month after month. Who. Who is, I am coming to believe, a bad child. Who turned, the way a rubber tyre turns, away and away and away. With success as a function of distance, who fell for the hum of wheels on asphalt. Who can sometimes only sleep on moving buses. Now I live across at least 5000 miles of land and sea, and still I never call. As a child, I used to think the full moon an occasion, an event that merits wonder. Waxing, waning were like myths or sacred processes. But I guess I thought this oversentimental, or maybe time moves faster now. Now the full moon comes here monthly. Returns before I'm ready to appreciate it. Texts come before I'm sorry for how long it takes to answer them. I used to fantasize about the moon. Sometimes lover; always saviour, who would drop into the window from the black sea of the sky and curtain me in grey. Now I work part-time in a café far too fast for any human small talk, and I write like I am losing something. Like a business. Like progress, or a road across a bridge across a hollow childhood. Like I want to call home, but. At the fixed speed of 60mph, a car's tyre turns about 800 times a minute, such that any given point on the tyre makes contact with the tarmac every 75 milliseconds. I can't find a word to stem the space I pour between myself and others. How long does cement take to dry? From this fixed point on the tyre, the stars are white and yellow lines. The moon is full again. The road is passing underneath me.

Colouring Book

In the waiting room, a child is spilling
her orange marker outside the lines,
concentrated and systematic, as if
the black and white Belle isn't there
and the page is blank. The way land
looks on a globe, there is a network
forming, a relationship between matter
and the open space around it, like how
I'm an Aquarius, and the parts of me
that correlate are too many to be just
coincidence, but not enough for me
to understand the bigger picture.
My hair's been coming out in patches;
stress compounding alopecia. Growing up,
I saw colouring as a test, dexterity
predicting concentration, futures
where I grew up clean and trim, so
my hands shook and I always failed.
I didn't know you could ignore
the lines. But there's a sort of gravity
to the way this girl fills the page; feng
shui with a puddle pooling, soaking
capillary up into the fabric of the dress,
and the patches' paradigms are shifting,
fungal how the marker's orange is growing
systems, nations – fissures in the lines
that show us how to sketch a princess.
I know some hair is never coming back,
same way I know that there's a pair
of hands shaping my life that I will

never really understand, same way
I know that I'll forget again and then
catch it on my way out in the mirror,
go back to grab a hat.

Bald

for Abbie

That first time, I presented you my hemispheres,
my globe, as though defeated. No one but you
had seen my head without a hat for months now,

but in the bathroom's ugly light, my scraggy scalp
was too exposed, the very air like forceps. I pictured
mapmakers in your pupils, documenting my head's

irregular topography, noting scraps and tufts, the pale
spaces where it'd begun to look like nothing ever grew.
I shuddered. We were quiet. Then the razor's buzz,

controlled steel-burn, electric brush fire, and soon
I felt the curls pooling in my lap. You were steady,
gentle fingers guiding, combing, unfazed to touch

this part of me that felt so like a wound, unfazed
to delve into the raw of it. When my head was smooth,
brand new the way that hope is new, you kissed me

like you'd always kissed me. And when I said I looked like
Caillou, femme Steve Harvey, you laughed, the ripple of it
cool and musical, smile swimming in the bathroom mirror.

Upon Leaving My Labyrinth

for Abbie

Summer outside. You are noble gorgeous
Theseus and I am. You are filled resplendent
with all the glory strength of Athens and I
am. Minoan sun blue like I've never seen.
Waves and water blinding heaping light
amnesia and the width of your arm the sand.

Flowery. You are heartstrong hourglass
noble Theseus you carry me like something
willless sunburned. There's something
softly sanguine in submitting. You
are Theseus noble soft expansive
whimsical I am asking hero will your

great ocean body hold me like this
buoyant. Will you hold me let me
lose what I've been what I'm waiting.
Small. Theseus. Power only in you only
in those dimples made benevolent. Something
deep safe to lose myself. Theseus look I.

I know you're only. I know mortality
vulnerable soullost I know we're all
like me look. I know. I've been asking
for God Goddess mother saviour I can see
how selfish God don't you think I.
I grew up reading books where knights

white horses princess towers. & I.
I know it's selfish but I'm asking
carry save me, simple heartsmall
summer blackboy that I am. I know
you want to be a God so please just
can you. Leave me buoyed Godheld guiltless

found for fucking once. Theseus.
Today lover please will you act my
archetypal Goddess will you let me
selfish lovely yours. Lover on this
open sunspun beach let me. Can I
for this minute stop existing in your.

III.

Every space you occupy is public space, that is, space which is definable by everyone. That is, the image which emerges from the Door of No Return is public property belonging to a public exclusive of the Black bodies which signify it. One is aware of this ownership. One is constantly refuting it, or ignoring it, or troubling it, or parodying it, or tragically reaffirming it.

— Dionne Brand, *A Map to the Door of No Return*

We burst into the scene defying expectation and they say we are animals. And we are animals, of a sort, lighting up cities with rage and tigers around our necks.

— Dawn Lundy Martin, 'A Black Poetics: Against Mastery'

Ariadne

after Deborah Tall

I imagine it began like this:
sea birds returning bearing

hints of music in their grating
calls. *Set out.* Quiet at first.

Until their beady eyes became
an accusation, until she started

seeing longing in the air that held
their wings. *Set out. Even a child*

knows how. In case she thought that
leaving might be difficult, just in case

she'd started thinking setting out alone
was something noble. Each morning,

she felt it scratching, eating at the palace
stone before she even opened up her eyes.

And then all day the island stung
with it, as if this feeling was a wound

that she could only dress in open water.
Set out. In her dreams, a voice told her

it didn't matter where, while the stars cut
yellow cracks into the sea's obsidian.

Sometimes she'd go to sit atop the cliff
that seagulls roost in, up where their screams

made sweet cacophony. Here, where the air
would crackle with the impetus for flight.

Saturn

after Stevie Wonder

According to the news,
it's visible to the naked eye
tonight. Golden dimple
in the night's dark skin,
near the constellations
Pegasus and Pisces.
There are a couple
clouds, but still we
go outside and make
a ceremony of squinting,
eyes following our index fingers
across dark and beds of pinprick
freckles, arms extended, faces
flushed with wind, pointing
into blackness deep as
centuries. Like hope,
like we're reaching
into dreams, like the lines
our index fingers draw can
save us. In space, Sun Ra saw
his origins, saw peace and altered
destiny. On Saturn, Stevie Wonder saw
a world where Black life expectancy
extends beyond two hundred,
where the air is clean and
there's no need for war.
Finger pointed upwards,
outwards, into Blackness.

The only way I know to phrase
this feeling: if I had a late-night
show, I'd use this song to end it; let
my viewers carry it with them to bed.

On Luther

Sometimes I think I'm just like him:
childish, selfish, however well-
intentioned, self-cast tragic hero.

To be fair, he's in a job for boys
with Batman fantasies, so he's not
the only cop who sees the world
as an old west saloon showdown
between good and evil, himself
an Atlas holding all the world's
order on his shoulders. He's not

the only dirty cop, although he is
the only one his colleagues treat
like they treat criminals. *The man
is nitroglycerin* they say, when really
what they mean to say is *Black*.
That's why he's so captivating:
ripping himself apart in service
of a system that would gladly
do it for him. *Noble*, we say.

Me, I foolishly believe that words
can wing me towards the sun;
that the only waves I'll ever make
will come after my inevitable fall;
that some of us are born for tragedy.
That like every story about Black
artists wrapped in whiteness, my lot
in life is trying nobly, dazzlingly –

burning out. I've never seen
a future for myself that didn't
end the way a firework does.

PLAQUE: AUTHERINE LUCY FOSTER

First African American to enroll at the University of Alabama following successful litigation under the historic 1954 Brown v. Board of Education ruling. She began classes on February 3, 1956; however, after three days of tumultuous demonstrations, on February 6, she was suspended and later expelled by the university's Board of Trustees. The expulsion was rescinded in April of 1988. In December 1991, Ms. Lucy completed the requirements for her master's in elementary education. This achievement was the culmination of her original dream to attend the University of Alabama and paved the way for countless others to fulfill theirs. Autherine Lucy's courage made the University of Alabama truly 'one for all.'

– Plaque on UA campus

After Brown v. Board of Education and following successful litigation, Ms. Lucy began classes at the University of Alabama. Ms. African American. First. The dream of her began three days of demonstrations. Tumultuous, *one for all* demonstrations. Demonstrations for expulsion, for the American dream, for ruling education. For the University of Alabama. After three days, she was suspended. Litigation. Culmination: the historic expulsion of the first African American. Later, after her dream, after demonstrations, after her achievement, after after, in 1988, the expulsion was rescinded. The university's dream. In 1956, she was courage suspended, achievement rescinded. She began and made the demonstrations, and she was the demonstrations. Completed the requirements for expulsion. She was Ms. Tumultuous. In 1991, she was *one for all* historic. Ms. Alabama, Ms. American. Courage to attend the university. Following successful litigation, the university paved the way.

Ode to Autherine Lucy

Twenty-six, you never meant
to be a movement. It was Pollie
who was set on symbols,
you who had to let yourself
become a battleground, ground
into the kind of words they throw
at you like bricks, even when they
claim to celebrate you. Bless you
for those three days, for the eggs
and riots and the grown men's
bright-red faces spitting threats
of worse. And bless your fear.
Through all the things they said
they'd do to you, how you held so
steady, like a promise. You were only
there to learn. Bless your schoolday
business, how alone you went about it,
how you starched your dress and how
your coat your hair your hands your
posture how you stayed so *dignified*.
Narrowed eyes like demonstrations
on your back, and still you stayed
three days. Above all, bless
the way you owned the thing
they didn't want to give you.

At my angriest, I'm a Black supremacist

I know that purity is just another trick,
but let us have it long enough to abuse it.
Put us on a pedestal, then justify it later.
Divine right, manifest destiny – anything.

It's high time we're misrecognized as saints,
or chosen ones, or goddesses, or whatever
Emerson believed that Anglo-Saxons were.
If you feel that we must be constricted,

do it with Chanel gowns, with tax loopholes,
with legacy admissions. I'm talking monuments
you fight to keep. Crimes you dig and dig
to see the good in. Worship the Atlantic

for the ancestors you laid to rest in it; plant us
on the moon like flags. Treat us like the nations
you believe in, whose ideals are grandiose enough
to remythologize whole systems, economies

grown from subjugation. I want to be ashamed
of all the resources you pull out of the earth
for me. I want to lie awake at night afraid
I didn't earn them. Before we abolish oligarchy,

give my grandmother a turn. Pledge allegiance
to the gap between my two front teeth.
String yourselves up from the sycamores,
the oaks, the elms, and wait for us to choose

to cut you down. Let us be so delicate
we're almost sorry; so alive we dance
on fault lines, dance in suburbs, public
transport, parking lots. Let us fall, get up,

and fall again. Make excuses for us;
musicals. Tell anyone who asks
that we're not perfect, but we give you
something to believe in. Love us

till we're tired of being precious. Carve
our founding mothers into mountains;
let their faces launch a thousand
acts of service. Call that reparations.

Self-Portrait as the Form of Other Jumpers

i. Ivan Ukhov

Sore winner, I have been known to wallow
in my better facets, suck out, savour the marrow
of my positives. Hammer, hone my prettiness
until it's sharp, becomes its own evidence.
I've always had a tendency to genuflect in front
of what I see as undeniable: Pelé making form,
technique an art, getting so good that no one
could deny him wonder, beauty just for
beauty's sake. Sure, what's the fun of being
good if you don't get to stop and bathe in it?

ii. Stefan Holm

You are at your most practical
when you find yourself with less
to work with. Over-serious.
When the margin is so small
between machine perfection
and the lowest benchmark
that you can afford to meet,
you need to narrow, turn
yourself into a textbook,
seek beauty only in the parts
of you that translate to precision.
Find pleasure in the simple,
in that which never strays
outside of brutal tidiness.
This calculus is nothing
personal – it behooves you
to quiet that which strains
against this winnowing.

iii. Javier Sotomayor

I'll admit: at times I prize my smoothness
over all other enlightenments; find that
there is satisfaction to be had at fitting
into grooves. I live for moments when
this magic happens without thinking,
for example, songs that script, direct
my movement with their bass, draw me
into pocket moments where I see myself
outside my inner criticism, can remove
the glasses of my double consciousness
and dance. Live only in that dancing.

On learning that my grandmother's great-grandmother Elmira, emancipated at 35, lived to be 102, to know my grandmother

In baseball, they say that the ball
is an extension of the throw, which
is itself a transfer of the body's
energy. A good pitcher follows
through, launches forward, having
given the ball a piece of herself.

The same can be said, of course,
of ancestry, that everything I am
I owe to history; my spirit,
my trajectory beginning centuries
before me. That we – my siblings,
my cousins – are the ball,
our momentum only an extension
of my great-great-great-grandmother's tenacity.

In which I attend my own lynching

I will be the first of the summer.
In the field, there are wildflowers swollen

with recent rain, and we are careful not to blot out
specks of pink and white and yellow with our shoes

and picnic baskets, though we must all find
the space to gather around the same tree:

old walnut with the long limb like a forearm,
knot of branches like the gnarled hand of God,

the dangling, empty rope all frayed and prickled.
My neighbour has brought grapes, cherries to sate us

while we wait for the procession to arrive.
Someone else has a punnet of strawberries,

and we do not mind the juice, the red and purple,
dripping from our lips, our chins, onto the cotton

of our collars, our Sunday dresses' necklines,
though we dab it from our children's mouths

with napkins. My high school headmaster
is here; my math teacher; my sister's classmate;

my grandfather's ghost. When I see myself appear
over the hill, I am bloody, carried by a crowd

of men in white, and the sun is just beginning
to make its bed on the horizon. The light

is syrup – still too early in the year
for fireflies, though it feels like an evening

they would hang above the grass to visit.
There is something building in the air,

a buzz, as others come with firewood.
We know it is more enjoyable if the bonfire starts

when I'm alive, when there are noises left
to draw from me, with the smells and blood

and souvenirs. We know this is meant to be
Dionysian. Bacchanal of cruelty. No one

will rush to save me. This is, of course, the point.
Godless, I must learn to see the sense in this:

the fingernails in flesh, the tearing. Be penitent,
give in. Because yes, I have been bad, wanted

too much, and I am far too flighty, selfish,
difficult, to be a proper lover, friend, or citizen,

so here I lend a hand to help my nation.
This is a symphony, and what am I

but instrument? What is my body
but an invitation? As the dusk chars

and the flames grow angrier, we begin
to fling the pieces of my face and chest

from us like sparks, let the lesser animal of me burn
comets, constellations, in the crumpled linen of the night.

Joni Mitchell dresses up as me (II)

When she leaves me in a pile
at the end of her bed, turns back
into herself for sleep, I up and walk
the streets, the jagged jazz clubs, alleys
of the white imagination, trail smoky
grace notes in my wake. Dance with
other muses, bodies, curios, on break
from metaphor: Saartjie Baartman back
from endless exhibition; the Zealy seven
cut, emancipated, from daguerreotype: Alfred,
Renty, Drana, Fassena, Jack, Jem, Delia; Caliban,
Othello. We end most nights with candles, whiskey
tumblers, playing cards at bars with little tables
where we laugh off all that makes our eyelids
heavy, stay for hours in the minutes before
morning dawns. Part with kisses on both cheeks,
reminders of the kind of love that stains us
lipstick-red, until we see ourselves again.

Tonight, the spire of the Forest Lake Baptist Church is the most beautiful thing I've ever seen

for Annika

sharp, tomb-white, spear-like, as it is
against late day's palatial body; sewing
needle into velvet. Clouds angelic, fractals
of concentric softness, recast here
as decoration. Newly, it is hard for me

to separate this beauty from its institution, sight
from domineering symbol. We are looping
one last time around this neighbourhood,
before our orbits take us outwards; starless
nomad planets we are soon to be. Ducklings,
last litter of the summer; trees in rosy
second bloom; porches, porch lights,
and the lives they broadcast;

and helpless, I am ready now to scrape my knees
in prayer. The amber of our final afternoon
has passed us, left us somewhere different;
pastoral shade of shipwreck we haven't seen
before; what wreckage looks like
when we're on our way to rescue,
as we leave the home and life
we built in lieu behind; first moment
back in open waters. Slowly, delicately,
we complete our loop, hang a second longer
at the edge, before tomorrow comes to meet us.

Theseus and the Minotaur

Yes, of course my maze is partly metaphor,
and of course my mind is also full of prisoners
and tunnels and a past I can't escape from –
even oceans, nations away – but I'm tired
of saying it like it's some sort of revelation.

I saw this forecast in the darkness back then,
thinking I could best it – saw it in the monster's
stunning eyes. Even in the gloom they twinkled,
brighter somehow than my torch. Earthy brown,
like the walls, like the dirt, like his patchy fur,

but also like two brand-new suns; polished bronze
inevitable. In them he saw me as I was, recognized
another captive series of dead ends, yet another life
who'd leave his ghost here. Here we stood in silence;
we two mercenaries, we rats in someone else's lab.

IV.

We'd love to take some more photos for you, but we've gotta be in this dance. With all our friends, our ghosts, and the gods we love.

– Ntozake Shange, *Liliane*

Icarus

I was told once about erupting volcanoes, how sometimes
the steam from their cones melts the wings off birds,
how you can stand at a safe distance
and watch their skeletons fall.

I was told that it's beautiful –
sad, alarming, of course – but beautiful
to watch them almost evaporate.

What goes through a bird's mind
in that last instant before the steam,
before its mind and body split?

Does it see the steam,
the shimmer in the air ahead,
and choose, still, to keep flying?

And when the steam keeps rising,
as you know it does, without the bird,
does it take the wings with it?

Fosbury Flop

His father taught him how to fly,
or at least how to prepare for it.
There were the exercises, chest

and back and shoulder strength;
the posture: ribcage like a ship's
prow, how to hold his body still

enough to flap the way a bird
does. They'd dissected them
together years ago, and Dad

had made him practise saying
pectoralis. Supracoracoideus.
Moved the swallow's drooping

wings first down and then back
up. He'd even learned to sketch
the arrowheads their bodies make

in silhouette against the evening;
pinprick beaks, their feathers' satin
ruffles in the daylight. Parabolic tails.

He wanted to go further, document
and map their curves, come up with
equations for their corkscrews, dives,

and cartwheels. This was more than
what they needed, but he dreamed
of a solution that could place his

consciousness between their black
gem eyes, let him feel force like beads
of water sliding off his contour feathers.

When it was time, his father left the cliff
mechanically; jump-flapped like they'd
practised, like a breaststroke swimmer.

But Icarus stepped back to give himself
more room to run. When he hit the border
between air and land, he turned and flung

his body backwards, chest out broad
just like his father taught him, blooming
skyward, like a diver in the early stages

of a backflip, like the swallows he'd seen
spiral, arrow bodies brushstrokes, masters,
how they'd always trust the air to hold them.

Inis Meáin

for SJ, Charlotte, & Ellen

Before the cottage, before the daisies in the grass, before
the narrow roads, before the fields cut into compartments

by the rocks and lichen, like a scalp divided phrenologically;
before all this, the harbour. Off the ferry, with our groceries

and luggage, we are waiting for a ride we hope is coming.
The concrete dock, all right angles, is empty but for us,

and we spread ourselves under the cautious sun, start in
on the cans we've brought along. Our first trip together,

we are slipping layers from ourselves like jackets, dangling
our feet over the water's edge. From the ferry's upper deck,

rocking, tasting salt, we could only talk about the power
of the ocean, its body like obsidian in flow, its cold a sort

of muscle. The fear that comes from wonder. But here,
uncorked, the four of us are crystalline with whimsy,

and the now-blue tide is stretching outwards. There are
walls of rock armour on the other edges of the harbour,

concrete in the shape of massive children's jacks.
With water as our backdrop, we begin to open up

our poetry. I tell them I'm afraid of how predictably
I structure mine, or the way my language piles like taffy,

how this bodes for a first collection. SJ pulls out Siken,
and we study how the lines embrace the fullness

of the page; space relations that can speak
to something innate, outside language. Then readings

of our own. A picture of the Barnard campus, or medals
on the necks of prizewinners. Our ambitions bare

in the Atlantic wind that tears across the island's
austere face; the stones and waves of wild grass.

High Jump as Icarus Story

Just inside the track's concentric
circus rings, at the football field's
head, is where I learned to wear
the gaze of other people like a queen
wears feathers. Meets, with everybody
watching, were the only times
I over-performed, always sharper
than in practice, always stronger,
faster, higher. I took this as a sign
from heaven: every step
in service of my flight was
blessed. I was going to leave
this self someday, construct
myself a new one in a world
where I wasn't so constricted.
The gods were mine to challenge,
mine to rearrange. Picture me vain
with self-mythology, sweeping,
like the all-commanding breath
of spring, across red polyurethane,
about to do what humans shouldn't.
When I started moving, everything
would fall away behind me; nowhere
else was this true. I choked on sax solos
in band, in math competitions, in soccer
when I had my chance to shoot. Yet here,
somehow, pressure was a drug I could
metabolize. In this updraft, I was floral,
inches from the height my dream school
wanted. I'd frayed my hamstring and it wasn't

healing, but surely my ascent was fated. It had been this way a while, and the doctor said he couldn't understand how I'd been running, much less flinging myself more than six feet in the air, so surely I would find a way again. Even at my last meet, when I felt my magic leave me – third place, out at 6'4" – I never saw my failure coming.

·

Oil Painting of a Hand Holding a Taxidermied Bluebird

Centre-right: wings invisible, pinned
like buttoned jackets round a waxdrop
body; small-clawed feet fixed perch-ready,
pointing out the painting's south-left corner,
down past the wrist. Human death delivered
stiffness, at the cost of first death's stillness,
between some hand's thumb and dull-white
forefinger, against the background beige, but

the show lights and the painter's chiaroscuro
leave the simple, broken body
almost princely; feathers soft-edged,
saturated; and the glint of gallery lamps
returns something, not-quite-but-almost sunlight,
to the soil-black shimmer in the single open eye.

How Planes Land

At the Southwest Airlines counter,
my bag is 6.7 pounds overweight.
Thankfully, Dad is there –
he parked and came in with me.
He says he'll take the excess weight
back with him, maybe mail it to me later.

While the whole line looks on,
I pull the zipper around the suitcase,
hesitate before lifting the top.

I have to decide again – here, now –
what is and isn't worth bringing:
the seven or so books I can't travel without,
my comfort sweater – maybe a second sweater
might be too many.

From the gate, I take note
of how planes land: wheels always pause
for a moment, waiting – hanging – inches
above the runway, reluctant.

When they take off, they do it
recklessly, tails shaking
like cats stalking prey, then

sprinting, accelerating,
as if they never plan on stopping.
From the terminal window, this looks careless,

but minutes later, flattened
in my seat by this same motion,
I feel safer than I ever have.

Landscape with a Wandering Icarus

National Gallery of Ireland, 3 February 2022

At the gallery, there is a wing,
up a Georgian staircase, hemmed
with gold-framed portraits. Lords,
earls, countesses with greying wigs
and eyes that look everywhere
in the room but at me, no matter
where I move.

        But among the careful-
ruffled gowns and measured stoicism,
there is a mirror here, and just like
those of servants in the backs
of regal paintings, my reflection's
eyes are there to meet with mine,
folding inward like the scenery
in landscapes

        fisheyes wide enough
to make their tiny people witnesses
to a world so much grander
than themselves, camped out
awestruck in their corner, seen
and seeing.

        I imagine them
expatriates in exodus, searching
for a country they'll be pictured in,
eager to ink their colour to a nation's

skin. I am photographed here
on my birthday, on the marble
staircase to the gallery of portraits,
grand and self-important.

those who are able to graze the sky, he believes,
must be gods

quique æthera carpere possent
crēdidit esse deōs

                    – Ovid, *Metamorphoses 8.219–220*

I've always wanted to build
a house of cards, but I don't
have the steady hands for it.
The way a man on a tightrope
swallows all the open space
between two cliffs; this sense
of turning self to spectacle
on one's own terms. I came close
to this a couple times, at the end
of high jump competitions when
I found myself the only one left
standing. My name came bubbling
through the stadium speakers,
and for a moment all the track-
meet-goers' eyes converged
on me. Alone, already having
won, I could ask the judge
to set the bar wherever, and
I got a final three attempts.
The tradition was to go
for greatness at a height
I'd never cleared, enlist
the whole track in a brush
with godliness. I don't think
I ever cleared a height this way
– with the echo of accelerating

claps marking each step,
the quiet that bloomed to fill
the stadium in the moment
after I took off – but I remember
always feeling triumphant,
precious, as my contorted
body fell back down, having
reached for sunlight,
even if I failed to hold it.

notes from my first big reading

i.

this is the part   in shakespeare's

comedies   where all the cast   returns

to dance   pretend the events   of the play

      were a dream   it is summer

the roof of the tent   is meringue   blackbird

song   and daisies   and the kind of grass

that only grows   from months of rain

       i am on stage   reading poetry

    and   we are crying   i am crying

         feathered   petals

    i've been waiting for a moment like this

    for years   for years relief is falling

     floral sprouting   on the stage top

the best movies   send their heroes

     sideways so that   what they achieve

often lives next door   to what they wanted

these movies end   intangible   less

fulfilment of a dream than   the suggestion

     that our hero finds   the thing

that hints   towards happiness

or to a cocktail   of feelings   that includes it

ii.

     if this is   a wedding   it is one between

     my hippocampus   and the feeling   that i'll be

     okay   airborne flowers   grace notes and

the way   smoke's twisting means   movement

     in the air around it   i can only name

this moment   using words   the wind displaces

my comedy will end   like this

      summer party   hopeful

         birdsong   friends

            dancing

From a West Cork Farm in Winter

When I text you 🛢 I mean the darkness
pouring through the cracks between my
curtains is primordial, and I'm afraid
of it, though I don't want to be. I mean
I wanted to embrace this, nestled between
hills, among the kind of green that feels
ancient, but I am beginning to feel stuck.

When I text you 🚜 I mean the machinery
that keeps my life in motion has gone rusty.
Yesterday, I used a vacuum to kill spiders,
heard the ugly *thwack* their bodies made
when the hose's suction caught them, can't
stop hearing it. I am waiting for news about
applications, and so far everything's been no.

When I text you 🏃 I mean today I walked
until the sun set, let the light desert the fog
before I started making my way back. No
street lights on the narrow road, so I jumped
into the underbrush each time I came across
a pair of headlights. Sheep bleating somewhere
in the distance, and my cell phone flashlight.

When I text you 🍲 I mean we work mornings
in the rain, planting, washing, digging, chopping
in our coats and wellies, and then come in mid-
afternoon for lunch of bread and cheese and soup.
Sometimes we are in the stables mucking out or

94

cleaning storage sheds, but mostly we are learning,
like the goats, to move untouched by weather.

When I text you 🌑 I mean mountain lakes,
like the one we hiked to in the day's last light,
stood up to our knees in, scraped our legs
through gorse to get to. On the way back,
we were luminous, like we'd washed away
our need for purpose in the muddy water,
like we could live in wonder's maw forever.

When I text you 🏔 I mean we get up for yoga
every morning, cup of tea and dress in thermals,
take the hour practice on our mats for waking
up. We alternate between two, which we call
standing and *sitting*, switch each weekday.
When we start out for the day's work, now,
we are bringing something extra in our steps.

When I text you 🏠 I mean, despite myself,
that I have settled in, burrowed deep into
the rhythm of my days. Another no last night,
but I am taking these in stride. When the rest
had gone to sleep, I went out in the starless
night and sang. In the wind and rain, my voice
was patient, gritty, though I doubt it carried.

From Here I See Tomorrow

How the sea's lip meets the land at high tide,
flat against this wall of rock. No beach, no middle
ground – just land and then, a centimetre later,
sea. The seam where the two meet sloshing
like bathwater. To step from one world straight
into another. Tectonic states of being. A boy
is running for the train that runs along beside
the water, tumbling wheels needling train-track
stitches. Out a bit, sailboats are racing; wind like
light we cannot see, or do not look for, metabolic
in a lush ecology of canvas, smooth as night-time.

Notes

'grendel' borrows a line from Laura Marling's 'Wild Fire'.

'What I Would Have Wanted *Fleabag* to Say for Me, Had the Priest Not Brought It Back to Sex' is written in reference to the titular character's confessional monologue in *Fleabag* season 2, episode 5.

'Joni Mitchell dresses up as me' is written in reference to Joni Mitchell's blackface alter ego, whom she called 'Art Nouveau' and who appears on the cover of her album *Don Juan's Reckless Daughter*. Joni once told *LA Weekly* that: 'I don't have the soul of a white woman. I write like a black poet. I frequently write from a black perspective.'

'Ariadne' borrows a line ('Set out – / even a child knows how') from Deborah Tall's 'Mountain Road', from her posthumous collection *Afterings*.

'those who are able to graze the sky, he believes, must be gods' is my poetic translation of a line from Book 8 of Ovid's *Metamorphoses*.

Acknowledgements

Grateful acknowledgement is made to the editors and staff of the following publications, in which the following poems first appeared, some in earlier versions:

32 Poems ('Upon Leaving my Labyrinth', 'Rococo'), *The Adroit Journal* ('Bald', 'those who are able to graze the sky, he believes, must be gods', 'After Practice, a Black Boy Goes Supernova'), *Banshee* ('Tortoise', 'High Jump as Religious Calling'), *Belfield Literary Review* ('Theseus and the Minotaur'), *fourteen poems* ('High Jump as Icarus Story'), *Frontier* ('Ariadne'), *Guernica* ('Diversity Statement'), *Indiana Review* ('Joni Mitchell dresses up as me'), *JMWW* ('Landscape with a Wandering Icarus'), *London Magazine* ('High Jump as Flow State', 'High Jump as Divination'), *The Missouri Review* ('In Which I Dream that I Sing like Lianne La Havas'), *Passages North* ('Saturn'), *phoebe* ('Oil Painting of a Hand Holding a Taxidermied Bluebird'), *Poetry Ireland Review* ('Quickly and Quietly'), *Propel Magazine* ('Lunar Cycle'), *The Stinging Fly* ('Tonight, the spire of the Forest Lake Baptist Church is the most beautiful thing I've ever seen').

'Rococo' also appears in *Romance Options: Love Poems for Today*, a 2022 anthology of contemporary love poetry published by Dedalus Press.

A selection of poems from this collection was shortlisted for the 2023 Listowel Writer's Week Poetry Collection Award.

Thank you to Stanford University's Chappell Lougee Scholarship and Levinthal Tutorial Program, the Ronald E. McNair Graduate Fellowship at the University of Alabama, the Obsidian Foundation, and the Irish Arts Council's

Agility Award for their generous support over the years, making this path possible for me.

So much gratitude to the friends who have been generous and encouraging readers for me as I put this collection together: Charlotte Buckley, Kevin Chappelle, Sophie Clark, SJ DeMatteo, Delany Lemke, Bebhinn McInerney, Niall MacMonagle, Annika Reitenga, Josh Sackett, Leela Srinivasan, Kaushika Suresh, Gwen Williams, Alissa Wolenetz. Much love, too, to Synergy, Okada, and LSJUMB.

Thank you to my Obsidian tutors, Raymond Antrobus, Malika Booker, Victoria Adukwei Bulley, Nick Makoha, and Dante Micheaux. And so much love to Obsidian Group D, who taught me to believe in workshops again.

Thank you to Richie Hofmann, who decided I was going to be a poet before I knew I could be.

Thank you to Ross Gay, who made sure I knew I belonged in the world of writing.

Thank you to Camille Dungy, for seeing me when I really needed to be seen.

Thank you to my PhD supervisors, Kevin Power and Rosie Lavan, who've been so supportive of me pursuing poetry adjacent to (and sometimes at the expense of) my studies.

I'm so grateful to my friends, families (Hibbetts and McLakes), and communities, without whose love, support, and belief I wouldn't have found my way here. Thank you for seeing me through all the twists, turns, and dead ends.

Thank you to Seán Hewitt and Victoria Adukwei Bulley for their generous, insightful feedback on this collection during the editing process.

Thank you to Laura Cassidy and Eimear Ryan for taking this collection on, and for welcoming me into the Banshee family.

Thank you to Anna Morrison for such a stunning cover.

Thank you to Jess Traynor for her care and patience in many, many rounds of edits, and for shaping this collection into something so much sharper, brighter, and fuller than when we started.

And thank you of course – always, deeply – to Abbie: my love, my home.

BANSHEE
PRESS

Banshee Press was founded by writers Laura Cassidy, Claire Hennessy and Eimear Ryan. Since 2015, *Banshee* literary journal has published twice a year. In 2021, Jessica Traynor joined Banshee Press as poetry editor.

The Banshee Press publishing imprint launched in 2019, publishing the very best in new fiction, poetry and memoir. Banshee Press authors include Bebe Ashley, Dylan Brennan, Lucy Sweeney Byrne, Mary Morrissy, Deirdre Sullivan, Rosamund Taylor and David Toms.

WWW.BANSHEEPRESS.ORG